MY FIRST Day of School

BY ALYSSA SATIN CAPUCILLI ★ PHOTOGRAPHS BY JILL WACHTER

SIMON SPOTLIGHT
NEW YORK   AMSTERDAM/ANTWERP   LONDON   TORONTO   SYDNEY/MELBOURNE   NEW DELHI

To fun-filled
students, teachers, and
classrooms everywhere!
—A. S. C.

Dedicated to all the young
students of life. Enjoy the
exciting new journey
that lies ahead!
—J. W.

SIMON SPOTLIGHT
An imprint of Simon & Schuster Children's Publishing Division
1230 Avenue of the Americas, New York, New York 10020
For more than 100 years, Simon & Schuster has championed authors and the stories they create. By respecting the copyright of an author's intellectual property, you enable Simon & Schuster and the author to continue publishing exceptional books for years to come. We thank you for supporting the author's copyright by purchasing an authorized edition of this book.
No amount of this book may be reproduced or stored in any format, nor may it be uploaded to any website, database, language-learning model, or other repository, retrieval, or artificial intelligence system without express permission. All rights reserved. Inquiries may be directed to Simon & Schuster, 1230 Avenue of the Americas, New York, NY 10020 or permissions@simonandschuster.com.
This Simon Spotlight edition June 2025
Text copyright © 2019 by Alyssa Satin Capucilli
All photographs and illustrations copyright © 2019 by Simon & Schuster, LLC
All rights reserved, including the right of reproduction in whole or in part in any form.
SIMON SPOTLIGHT and colophon are registered trademarks of Simon & Schuster, LLC.
For information about special discounts for bulk purchases, please contact Simon & Schuster Special Sales at 1-866-506-1949 or business@simonandschuster.com.
Simon & Schuster strongly believes in freedom of expression and stands against censorship in all its forms. For more information, visit BooksBelong.com.
Manufactured in the United States of America 0325 LAK
10 9 8 7 6 5 4 3 2 1
CIP data for this book is available from the Library of Congress.
ISBN 9781665972482
ISBN 9781534428461 (ebook)
This book was previously published with slightly different text and art.

Today is my first day of **school**.

I have my **backpack** and **lunch bag**, too.

Here is my **classroom**. I wonder what we will do!

Ms. Gray is my **teacher**. She greets us with a smile.

My things go in my **cubby**. Now I can play awhile!

I see **sand** and **puzzles**.

I paint at the **easel** too.

We build a **tower** to the **sky**,

Circle time is next.

We all sit together.

We hear about the day ahead.

We learn about the weather.

Recess time!

We go outside.

I like the swings.

The **nature table** is the place for a closer look at things!

Snack time! Snack time! We pour water and munch away.

Then we dress in **costumes**.

What should I be **today**?

At *story time*, I lead the *line*.

I **shake out my sillies** at music time.

Soon it is the end of the day.

"See you **tomorrow**," says Ms. Gray.

My first day of school was so much **fun**.

LET'S GET READY FOR SCHOOL

ASK A GROWN-UP TO HELP YOU READ MORE ABOUT WHAT HAPPENS AT SCHOOL!

WELCOME TO SCHOOL!

Your teacher is always there to welcome you and help you find your cubby.
A backpack or bag can hold a change of clothes and a healthy snack.
It is a great way to bring home the wonderful things you'll make at school too.

FREE PLAY

Are you ready to discover your busy classroom? At the sand table you can dig, pour, and build. At the water table you can guess which things will float and which things will not.

There are always lots of puzzles and books too.

Your classroom may have an easel or finger paints, or both! Be sure to put on a smock or apron first. Then paint away!

CIRCLE TIME

At circle time your teacher will tell you all about the day ahead. Soon you will learn the names of everyone in your class.

WEATHER STATION

Every day you will learn about the weather. You may even help the teacher with the weather chart! Your teacher may ask you if it is sunny, rainy, snowy, or windy outside.

OUTDOOR PLAY

It is important to get lots of exercise at school. At the playground you can run, climb, swing, and slide. There may be bicycles and toy cars to ride around and around.

What else can you do outside? You can find shadows and observe nature. A magnifying glass is a fun way to see a tiny bug grow bigger and BIGGER!

SNACK TIME

After a busy morning, it is time for a delicious snack. First you will wash your hands with soap and water. Then you can enjoy a healthy snack such as apples, cheese, raisins, or carrots with your friends. You can help pour water, milk, or juice.

WASH YOUR HANDS

To start, wet your hands with a little water. Then get some soap.
Rub your hands together. Be sure the soap gets on both sides of your hands and in between your fingers.
Next, wash off the soap with clean water. Then dry your hands with a clean towel.

PLAY PRETEND

Do you like to dress up? Find a funny hat and play pretend.

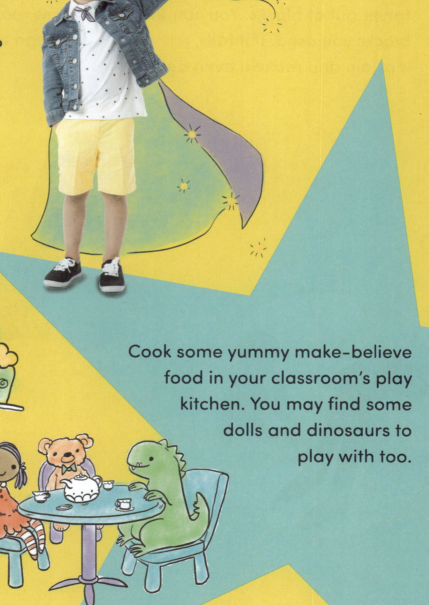

Cook some yummy make-believe food in your classroom's play kitchen. You may find some dolls and dinosaurs to play with too.

BUILD WITH BLOCKS

Calling all engineers! You can build a bridge or tower out of blocks. You can even count how many blocks you used. If it falls, it is okay . . . you can build it again and make it even better!

STORY TIME

At story time you can take a comfortable mat or cushion and listen to the teacher read a story or poem. Do you have a favorite book already?

MUSIC TIME

At music time the teacher may play the guitar or piano. You can sing, dance, and stomp along!

CLASS PET

Some classrooms have pets. If yours does, you may have a chance to feed your class's pet hamster, fish, or other animal.

THERE ARE SO MANY FUN THINGS TO DO AT SCHOOL.

You will make new friends and learn lots of things every day.

Which activity did you like best?

What was your favorite part of the day?

What would you like to try tomorrow?

SCHOOL IS COOL!